Pointing the Way Home

Rees Campbell

Pointing the Way Home

Acknowledgements

Some of these poems have been previously published.
'Soft love' in *Poetry d'amour* anthology, WA poets, 2014
'The sins of the fathers' in *The Legacy*, 2007
'Climate change' in *Poetry d'amour* anthology, WA poets, 2018
'My Island' in *Brazenly Pure,* 2012
'Perkins Island' in *The Paradise Anthology* 5, 2011; *Brazenly Pure,* 2012; and *One Surviving Poem,* 2019
'Hard stand – Albany' in *Blue Giraffe* 14, 2015

This selection of poems is written for those who have come from my life and who make my life – my husband and mate, Col; my children Niko, Rin, Jess and Loki, and their children. I'm sad for the poorer world we are leaving them.

Thank you (and sometimes apologies) to all those I have loved; those I love; and those whose love I have.

I am grateful to this island for its wonders.

Pointing the Way Home
ISBN 978 1 76109 170 4
Copyright © Rees Campbell 2021
Cover image: Sarah Smith
Author photo: Col Meyers

First published 2021 by
Ginninderra Press
PO Box 3461 Port Adelaide 5015
www.ginninderrapress.com.au

Contents

Love and Anti-love
- Impossible — 9
- Three times — 10
- The black dog man — 12
- Soft love — 14
- Asleep — 15
- Borrowed time — 16
- Tulip — 17
- The sins of the fathers — 18
- Dead finish — 19
- My mother — 21
- Losing a Parent — 22
- My grandmother — 24
- For Finn — 26
- Climate change — 27

Place
- I am yours — 31
- My island — 33
- Dead cider gums at Liawenee — 34
- They call it shifting baseline syndrome — 35
- Nine Grey Geese — 36
- Perkins Island — 37
- Seahorse at Montagu — 38
- The mountain speaks to me — 40
- The mountain — 42
- Hard stand – Albany — 43
- Warrego River Camp — 44
- Drought (2) — 45
- Just a Line in the Sand — 46
- Montagu Swan Song — 49

Other Things
  Old George 53
  Toby 57
  The Old Magnolia Tree 59
  Cunts and other conversations 61
  Valeria Ramirez 62
  Small-town Girl 64
  Change of Heart 66
  Claire Anne Taylor 68
  Home 69

About the Author 70

Love and Anti-love

Impossible

If I told you how heavy it is to carry
the cross; the intersection between
my nerves and my brain, my pain. The path
made treacherous and slippery
with the allure of morphine, misting
the view of gum leaves blowin' in the wind
without an answer
without a rhyme

If I told you of the wishes I throw
with pennies in the wells that disappear
soundless with just a twisting glint
of light that maybe
wasn't there at all

If I told you of the moment which is long
and short and forever, when I wonder
if today is the day I crumble
into sand

If I told you that your love
is a tightrope wire
an abseil rope
a towing line
a moonlight rainbow
could you bear it?

Three times

Three times I've truly loved a man
And three times have indeed been loved

While many love not even one
My loves have held me close and loved me well

But three loves flawed, crystals marred
A junkie, a black dog, and another's husband

My lover boy, father of my two babes
Sweet boy, couldn't bear to become a man
Wine, women and song too tempting
Reality held at bay with
Bottles and needles, mushrooms and dope

Had to leave, had to go,
and let myself and the children grow

Then my gentle man, the family maker
Provided for all and fathered two more
Toiled and worried, fretted and envied
Till he killed all the ease and all the joy
And the black dog bayed in victory

Had to leave, had to go,
had to breathe and make him let me go

And now, my lover man, my friend
The mirror to my soul
And the riser of my pulse
Speaker of all the words
I've always longed to hear

But I have to leave him loose
As he's not mine to hold
And one day, any day, he'll tell me
He has to leave, has to go

The black dog man

The black dog man loves
like only a black dog can
   with hopeless patience
and little expectation of return

The black dog man moves alone
sidling around the edges of lives and loves
not really knowing how to feel
not really feeling that he knows

I still try to restore
my black dog man
I talk of love and hate and commitment
words of pain and anguish, grief and joy

Words that drop
silently
onto the black dog's heart

I make love like a whore, a mistress
a lover and a wife
I hold him tight and whisper words of adoration
or throw him off with words of disdain and scorn
demanding a real man's response
but the black dog man just curls up and sleeps

Sometimes the black dog is obedient to the man
resting quietly close at heel

but the man's black dog gets hungry quickly
snaps at his heels and bays at the moon
then the black dog man
descends his lonely way
to a very personal hell
again

Soft love

In the world we make each night
of crumpled sheets
and dark huddle doona
over curled bodies quiet

When the cool moon stares
and the cormorants mutter quietly in the old dead gum
you turn to me with sleepy soft skin
and our bodies meld and blend
under the moon's bland gaze

Your work scuffed palm softly sweetly gently
follows the hip swoop dip over ribs to smooth swelled breast
curved under like the crescent moon
and we mutter to each other like the cormorants outside
gentle words of here now forever love

And with that touch
we fall asleep again holding hands
as the slow moon, drowsy with dawn
slips behind the silhouetted tree tops

Asleep

It makes me smile
and fondness swells
to watch my man in sleep.

Age has crept up on his head
as it lies disembodied on the pillow.
His hair is sparse now,
and his argument with the sun
is there in spots and patches.

His argument with the world is there
in dents and white stitch marks
but his brow is pink and peaceful
hiding thoughts and dreams that
make his eyes race behind the lids.

I can see right through his lashes
as colourless as a blonde baby.
He rarely talks or moves in sleep
but remembers those dreams
mostly of an era gone
of life in his old trawlers.

But often ploughing through the land
in a tense and anxious task
made sensible by the unconscious
I'm rarely in those dreams
but as soon as he stirs,

his eyes find mine
and it makes him smile.

Borrowed time

I once loved a man who wasn't mine
I borrowed him; a bit like
taking a library book from the shelf.
I knew he wasn't mine,
but once the book was opened
I fell deep into the story
entranced, bewitched, bedazzled
by the ways that man showed love.

We became a creature
with no end and no beginning
me the character and he the reader
his words brought me undone.
Him the character, and me the reader
my words brought him undone.
He came to me in the dawning pink
and in the dark of moonless nights
And man, that man could love.

We couldn't bear the book to finish
so we invented new chapters
an old story made new.
But when I put him back on the shelf
you couldn't tell it had ever been borrowed.

Tulip

He called it her tulip.
He would kneel before her,
in supplication and in thrall.
He would kiss her, then,
touch so gently those petals of deepest pink
those petals which would bruise
like flesh debased.
Caress the bud with love
till sunrise blush and
opening bloom.
Lick the dew drops as they form
and breathe deep
the earthy aroma of the oldest flower.

The sins of the fathers

An old man is dying
his brilliant mind, social conscience
and passion for life

Long-dead.

That razor tongue now blunt and bent
his heavy hand gnarled and useless

No mirror in life
ever allowed the man to know himself.
No truth impossible to overcome.

And though I want
a clean slate for myself
free from sins of judgement and pride

Unable to achieve an apology
unlikely to receive an acknowledgement

I'm unwilling to grant him absolution
and wish him only a day pass from hell.

Dead finish

A tiny stunted wattle Acacia tetragonophylla growing in inland Australia is known as Dead Finish and is used as a last resort feed by the cattle and kangaroos in severe drought. If this wattle dies, it is the end, the finish.

Dead Finish

The old man
bent and twisted in body as well as mind
slowly wanders the halls of the nursing home
and the emptying corridors of his brain.

Dreams are unkind to this most unkind of men
who thinks he is the doomed cruise ship
Marie Celeste, but long before she sank.
He hoots at strangers.

But all are strangers now
even those who are family
except occasionally, he sees in me
the woman who was his wife.

My mother died before her time,
and before this sick old man.
She plaintively cried, one long cold dawn
'Now I'll never be free.'

So my father, alone and lonely
shuffles and groans
while nocturnal monsters haunt
the vestiges of thought

that flicker through the fog.
He plaintively asks
'Do you think she loved me?'
'Yes,' I say. 'Once, she did.'

But the man who deliberately
hurt, both in body and in mind
all who loved him,
died unloved.

My mother

There was never uncomplicated laughter
from my mother's belly.
There was never unconditional love
from her arms.

Instead there was a shadow in her eyes
twisted in the spiral of smoke
cloaking her face
from the world.

The bones of her face
were straight and true.
Her beauty transparent.
Her pain was not.

Nine years ago she died. Quietly.
She never answered
those questions I didn't ask
and still hasn't.

Losing a Parent

Sounds a bit too careless.
Losing a parent.
Losing the person who gave me life,
made me
into who I am.

I didn't lose my mother,
although she did slip
slowly away from
life and living and breathing.
And me I guess.

But I'd have given her away much sooner
if it could have saved her
from how she fought
to die
in peace.

And now when you ask me
how I feel
about losing a parent,
I only feel
that she's not here.

Not a sense of loss
because I didn't lose her.
She died
as old and sick people
do.

And nothing like the pain
of losing love,
misplacing that feeling
that drives the world
and feeds the soul.

And nothing like the loss
of friendship
when distance or time or
the world gets in the way
of keeping friends
because there's always
the potential
of meeting again.

But my mother has died
and I watched her go.

My grandmother

She was old
when I was very young.
Her kingdom a garden
where raspberries were cossetted,
prickly stems tied and wired,
serrated into rows
dipping and bending with red treasures
best picked by commandos
crawling along shadowy paths
between armed columns
our legs a childhood design
of minute lacerations and ground in dirt.

She was old
when I was still young.
A yabby pond instead of fairies
at the bottom of her garden
where lumps of old meat tied to string
would reward your patience
with a fearsome creature swinging wild punches
from one pincer, the other holding tight
to the promised reward.

She was old
but I was growing up.
Repulsed and fascinated
by her flattened chest with
tiny saggy breasts that didn't need support.
Bras turned into handy pockets
for hankies and bits of string.
Her outdoor loo
a bravery trial at night
a faceoff with huntsmen and black house spiders
more at home than me
in this Halloween setting.

She was old
when I was grown
and had made her a great grandmother.
The earth had shifted on its axis
for us to connect.
I never thought I would wipe
that wizened wrinkled bum
her helplessness as grudging
as my help.

My grandsons glazed blue eyes
are hers.
And I grow raspberries all in rows.

For Finn

my grandson

I saw you –
in the furtive longing of your mother's eyes
long before I held you.

I felt you grow and kick,
the dreams of your mother and father
stretching with love to the moon and the stars

and back to the nest they were building
in the little old timber house.
I resisted being there at your birth,

that particular intimacy belonged only to your parents,
in the same way their love making had, I thought.
But how wrong could I be?

I watched as you stretched my daughter's body
almost out of possibility.
Watched as you finally burst through the wall of flesh
barring you from this world
in an ungodly rush of blood and birth water
splashing over my feet on the white hospital floor.

I comforted her in that moment of fear
before your bruised blue flesh flushed at first breath.
Your mother's cry bereft of all withholding,
her primal sound such a fierce
and pure rendering of love and possession.

My hands were blooded and my heart was yours.

Climate change

My sun shone in her eyes
my moon slept with her at night.
Her arms held out to me
showed how the whole world
is inside just one embrace.

Her tears ran down my flesh
her anger burnt my skin.
Her laughter and gentle words
were the clearest water
and a rainbow in the mist.

Her years passed and her bones grew long.
My love for her such a tree
I knew no storm could ever budge.
Her branches were mine, her journeys and adventures
a novel for me to read.

Her children borne, her man beside her
my daughter now my very best friend.
In a mirror, our reflection.
Years of gardens and goats,
of parties and happiness, a magic beach shared.

Now I look in the mirror
and the lone old woman looks back.
Her face lined like mud channels,
dwindling after floodwaters
washed the tree downstream.

Place

I am yours

in the flying triangles of eagle rays
feeding amongst the seagrass in the
green waters circling Robbins Island.

I am yours in the
Pacific gulls calling home
in the westerly wind.

I am yours
from the smallest of the million
soldier crabs dot painting in the sand
to the towering dolerite columns
rearing from the southern ocean.

I am yours
in the flames burning
on a robin's breast in winter
to the black-scaled one, coiled
warming on a granite boulder.

I am yours from
the blue sea star in the Bruny bays
to the black cockatoos
announcing weather changes in the mountains.

I am in the potoroo
feeding on the fungi
and I am in the wombat
feeding on the poa
and I am in the devil
feeding on the dead.

I am yours when there is no light save
the stars
I am yours when there is no sound save
the trees breathing
I am yours when there is no colour save
the waratah blooming in the snow.

You are in me when
I am nothing but a pebble on the shore.
You are in me when
I am nothing but birdsong in the bush.

I am in you, my island
and you are in me
with no ownership
just acknowledgement.

My island

It is when I tell you of the
moon on the silk-soft water
of the misty droplets jewel beading
berry red berries
in the running rock river

It is when the words I write
bring back the day
of the harsh laughing currawongs
glinting coin eyes
at what the world may offer

It is when the chosen photograph
traps the mist and frames the mountains
or prints a moment
the eye couldn't quite hold
in infinity

Dead cider gums at Liawenee

The moon is red tonight, my love
many thousand tides have waned
while we still stand, still bearing time
in mute protest of our demise

The moon is red tonight, light
shines unfiltered through our whitened limbs
starkly silhouetted
cleansed by death and time

Two hundred years and more
wounded both by black and white
for our sugared blood
that no longer runs from roots to leaves

The moon is red tonight, I fear
with bloodlust from the fires
that burn this old old land
back to the rock from which it came

With flames above and the devil's heat below
roasting this island and all that dwells

A cemetery of tortured shapes
we stand as silent witness
to a failing earth
while the red moon slowly circles

They call it shifting baseline syndrome

My grandmother
bent low by children
and the hanging boughs
chased a thylacine from the hens

My mother
tended her garden in neat profusion
read us stories
of sealers and piners

I, once, watched a mirage
with deep set jaws and stripey back
disappear through the trees
to the past

My grandchild is taken
to visit The Wall at Derwent Bridge
and pays to see huon pine boards
beautifully knifed into facsimiles
of what once was.

Nine Grey Geese

The stillness goes on forever
as sand meets sea meets sky
where basalt boulders bulge
like slumbering whales
in the silky shallows

Until nine grey geese
lumbering and honking
split the sky
and carve the day

Then they are gone
and the grey sky
heals seamless
and the stillness
returns

Perkins Island

Where birds are tilted by the wind
carving gaps in the air
and the swell breathes
the tide up and down, in and out

The whales lie still
in the grave they chose
if not the death

On the edge of a lonely land
where the sea is shallow
but the world breathes deep

Where a thousand thousand shells
sprinkle gems
on wind-scoured bleak

The whales' white bones
arch and curve
sad and strong
through waves of sand

Seahorse at Montagu

A perfect child's painting
the round yellow sun right at the top
of the pale blue sky

It was middle of the day in the
middle of summer
and the tide was out

They crossed the sandflats to the channel
distracted often, by baby flounder
flitting like coins in the shallow pools

By carnivorous snails loop-skitting
towards the scent of flesh
from a recently shed crab leg

By almost invisible shrimps
that fling themselves hysterically
into legs

At the water's edge
she knelt and tenderly
adjusted snorkel and goggle
of her grandson
temporarily silencing his chitter

They slipped into the warm water, headed for the
almost uncovered pile of rocks
ballast from a trading ship probably a century ago;
but now a splendid iceberg of tumbled habitat

Bumping blackly down
into the freckled light of the deeper channel
softened, covered now, in seaweed; a cloak of
brown and green disguise

Shifting and twisting
to display the
purple spined urchins feasting
the rounded shell of abalone
with the black lip and feelers peeking out

The tulip shell with bright red mollusc
hunting amongst the crevices
and there, way down there; with fluttering wings
the treasures…

Sea horses with curled tail clasping a frond
of brown and green like them
he dives, but disappointed, can't get the depth

She dives and snips the frond,
brings the sea horse, untroubled by the change of scenery
to him

And in the shallows of the channel
The boy sits, entranced
as the sea horse
curls its tail around his fingers
with the charming grip of a new babe.

The mountain speaks to me

of perseverance, tenacity,
of holding on to what is you
despite pummelling of rain, of snow
of beratings by the southern winds.
How a life well lived has a weathered face
of how the hot red rock rush-roaring from the
centre of the earth
becomes the cold red dirt, still and silent
growing prickly mountain heath
and the delicate native violet.

The alpine creek sings to me
in melody and harmony
of whirling dervishes of thought
and swirling depths of black despair.
How even a life well loved
has frothing backwaters of indecision,
of learning through the stories
told as we move through our lives
of the power that water
in constant motion through the landscape
or a single teardrop has.

The forest trees whisper to me
in their sibilant songs
of strength and togetherness
of the constant cycle of lifeanddeath.
A limb falls, rots, becomes earth again
while the wound becomes a home
for the pardalote to sing its three note song
again and again
whilst hidden in the canopy
and below the potoroo digs for fungi
and cultivates the humus
for a fern spore to take hold
and in time, in all the time it takes
a massive manfern grows

On the wing, a solitary currawong calls to me
of love and loneliness
of loss and joy and life
and as it flies towards the winter sun
the south wind steals the sound

The mountain

Snowflakes lilting, dawn
comes in black and white, snow clouds
darken everything

Hard stand – Albany

On hard-baked land they rest
where mermaid's song is a magpie's lie.
The prizes, with the corpses
propped on tired elbows
of steel, cement or wood.

With cracked and broken ribs,
or stove-in hull
these salvaged wrecks bloom rust
like cemetery wildflowers.

Yachts of yesterday
heeled no longer to the roaring forties.
Copper rovings and caulking hanging,
bowsprits askew
and rigging limp.

Old crayboats,
carthorses of the sea
with gaping wounds between planks
as wide as a fisherman's thumb.

Each ghostly frame a dreamcatcher
of challenges, adventures
and brave journeys to have begun.

While ravens, black as fate
climb the lugger's ratlines
and mock the folly of men
who dream to sail her again.

Warrego River Camp

On the way to the river
we passed an Aussie bloke
you'll recognise the sort – in his muddy once-white ute
with the blue heeler tied on the back.

His sunburnt elbow bracketed by the rolled up flanny
said 'G'day, mate, just gettin' a few roos' and drove on.
A minute later, a shot
punctured the afternoon.

Later, we sat quiet by the campfire
watching the winter sun relax
into a bed of pink and purple
as darkness swelled.

Like sorrow in grey
she came creeping soundlessly
with joey swollen pouch
from her shelter in the scrub.

Ignored the fire, ignored us
found the blood trail and followed
her mate's last heart beats
dripped on barren ground.

Stopped
and waited beside the cooling congealing pool
until darkness hid her grief

Drought (2)

2018

Exhausted, defeated; the emu
folds to the dirt
in an untidy origami of feathers

Even after the cattle were moved, then sold
after most of the mulga was pushed
in a Custer's stand of prolonging
the inevitable

The roos and emus, and those ever present
voracious goats picked an existence on the roadside
played a deadly roulette with hunters
and trucks and starvation

After moisture was only a shimmering memory mirage

And now, only the crows – jaunty
and glistening with fat eaten from the dead
circle like judges around this last emu
in her final, lingering hour

A rubbish pile of silver feathers
in a world of dry red sand
The crows strut officiously;
waiting for her head to sink

Waiting for her eyes.

Just a Line in the Sand

They came in a good year
when the grass shimmered green.
Men with vison and excitement
from England mostly, some farmers,
some just men with the blood for adventure
but not the money to buy it.

North they travelled
tramping over Goyder's line so carefully drawn
to new land released under Strangways Act
mostly on credit from the govmint, o' course.
Ten per cent down, the rest from the wheat
you'll harvest no doubt.

The only obligation
to live on the land till it was their own
so their women and children followed,
unwilling or willing, it was of no matter.

The rain was good this year the men said.
We can make a go of it here
striding through grasses stubbled with salt bush,
blue bush, mallee   easy land to clear.
They counted their bags of golden grain
long before it was sown.

Broke the mallee off, tore the bushes from the land
the only cover for miles around,
believed a god would send
rain to follow the plough.

And sometimes, for five or seven years, rain it did.
The wheat was reaped, the gold was counted.
Strong houses built from the stone of the land
by the hand of the men who hewed it,
a house as grand as the future they saw
and babies; two, three born.

But again, and again
that line in red stained sand
drawn by a man who could read the land,
who knew that salt bush and mallee
were children of the dust, not of the rain

sent men first to plough the dry
to watch the sky for years.
Finally sent them to their knees
to pray in vain.
Sent women to the graveyards
to tend mounds that marked their babes.

Tough men   weather-beaten.
The retreat was as inglorious as in war.
Men stooped by the weight of their folly
bent by the burden of failure
and their women worn thin and old.

And the land laid bare
bones of mallee
blowing the dust of dreams

and the cold wind of doom
blasts tumbleweed into corners
of fine stone houses
empty of all
but the view from the windows.

Montagu Swan Song

We sat on the jetty
that last time, the dog and I
she pointed her nose to the wind, ears blown back, Snoopy style
learning all the secrets the wind brought to her

That same wind my excuse for the tears
blurring my vision

I rode my ponies again, along the sand flats
cantering through a westerly fierce enough to escape their hoofbeats
mares' manes whipping here and in the channel
racing apart and away

I saw the seagulls pud puddling in the silty sand
forcing worms to the surface
then moving along, pud puddling again
a raggedly potholed path

I admired the stingray silhouettes
diamonds left by receding tide
a story of this day
filling and disappearing a few hours later

Amongst the samphire lands
and pools; each one a world
of flounder tidlings and see-through shrimps
rest and camouflage for speckled chicks

of oystercatcher and fairy tern
whose black and white parents
bring molluscs and silver fishlings
to pour down open throats

I found the rare and common crabs
under rocks and in the crevices
so many soldiers unmarshalled
a purple dot painting in the sand

I remember the children scampering, climbing
swimming amongst the rocks and the fish
learning this magic world
in the joy of summer sun

I saw the giant spider crabs entwined
in a macabre orgy of a million orange legs
making their bed
in the richness of the seagrass

And there beside them
the gently swaying seahorse
anchored softly to the weed
composed in repose

I lived again that frisson of fear
when the silky black tiger snake
reared but did not strike
though I'd wandered on his path

And the dog and I looked west
to the setting sun and the living water
to feeding swans; black with drops of red
their sadness hanging in the wind

Blowing my tears of memory
far away

Other Things

Old George

Sweat-slicked rope, his arms hemp tendons braided taut
the old fisherman rock-hewn.

Sunburnt sun-bleached sunbaked;
but morning sky eyes search horizons still
and his yarns, rising and falling with the sea
as scarred and barnacled as any keel,
the adventures strewn like treasured prawns in the sorting tray

leaving the rest to flop impotently in the fish stink of rubbish.
Brittle sea urchin spines snapping   crimson twigs without support,
sinuous stripes of sea snake   writhing
the parody of carousel with dainty sea horses suffocating
and a thousand sunrise-pink gold mollusc shells rejected.

Those dollars hard earned in boats hard built
of welded steel and coppered wood; in sparks and sweat
to challenge reefs and waves for bounty torn from coral seas.

*

Tragedy and trauma casually dismissed
in wry tales through decades of toil
gear hooked up and over she went
no time for plans – the deckie was swimming before he knew he
   was wet.

Upended in an endless black sea,
a full day's steaming from the land.
The old fisherman at ease in the wrath of the sea
but trapped by the lines that pulled the boat over and down
swam   up to the bottom of the boat
for that precious pocket of unspent air.
Breathed deep, and thought fast as the boat shuddered and wept.

Pushed back down through watery spaces
where fish already swim but a man needs air.
Three times, through the tangle of wires and nets,
past the wheel turning, turning nowhere

Till he reached the surface of a hostile sea.
An imposter.

And swam through all that fearful night
through the punishing sun and salt of a full and golden day
into the relief and terror of the next dark, they floated, drifted.

Talked each other through desperation
and that unholy fear when sharks circle the bait
and the bull sharks bump with lethal intent.

I'd been a diver and so I knew
that so long as a white didn't take me in half
it'd just be the bull sharks bumping and testing.
You fold your arms in, tuck your legs up – stay still in a foetal
  position
and they'll bump you to check, but you'll be all right, they won't
  bite.

And they were picked up.
Red and bruised and exhausted.
Swollen and split by the warm and salty sea.
Alive.

*

And the stories the others tell
when the old man leaves them gathered
around nets and hooks and bouys.
Of how he'd send his little boat to gouge ferocious storms
in search of prawn or scallop.
When lesser or saner men
would anchor boats in harbours and in ports.

And how he fought forever.
He fought the sea, he fought the fish,
he bruised the reef for profit
'cause in his time there was no end of 'product' to be caught.

I've seen the reefs repair.
It's bullshit, all this protection talk – there's product there for ever.
I used to trawl all night. Dump the rubbish off the edge in the morning
and start again near by
and go there a year or two later, you'd never know I'd been.

They tell of grief, of loss, of untellable guilt.
His wife, his son, his father all dead
with his own hands at the wheel.
Of finding no answers in the bottle,
so rising, burning, grieving, from his own ashes
to pillage the seas again and again.

And they also speak of adversity
of dogged bravery and a resilience
that marks pioneer and survivor
as surely as any tattoo of numbers on a forearm.

*

The old fisherman sits now with slow and aching bend.
Those hands are gnarls of knotted twine,
fingers tortured and knuckles swollen by time and tide.

A rusted wreck of the steel that was.

Toby

The cliché of painted silver skulls
on his sleeveless leather jacket
and his thick arms tattooed
with red hearts and blue girls.

A big bloke in the aisle seat
– of course –
and how many hours is it
across the Great Australian Bight?

Our conversation stutters
from destination to family
glimpses from my refuge in the novel
like a peep between venetian blinds.

His fear of flying burdens
my non-committal social responsibility.

Until suddenly there's a YouTube video
on his phone
of his heavy metal band
and there's the rhythm
heartbeat drumbeat

And did I know he was playing
at the Prince of Wales pub
only a coupla blocks
from where we're staying

Just ask for Toby
and they'll let you backstage
meet the mates
it'll be fun

But on Saturday night
we're tired, too tired.

I wonder how his flight back went.

The Old Magnolia Tree

Skinny scabbed knees drawn up
tight beneath her
she surrenders willingly
to the hard embrace
of the old magnolia's
gnarled and tangled limbs

Each leaving
she lightly touches
her scarred talisman
each return
she deeply breathes
the knowing of home.

In winter
it is as sad as she
tears dripping
and the world laid bare
there is nowhere to hide
so she waits.

But in spring there is promise
of softness
as the fuzzy buds rise anew
she rubs blushing petals
over her skin
imagining.

And then in summer
when the world is harsh
with sun and heat
the old magnolia hides her
for hours under the mosaic of leaf and light.
She dreams.

Cunts and other conversations

MONA exhibition, Hobart

I'd heard about you women
prepared as you were to put your labias on the line
to show us how we look
to turn young women
away from the mutilation of labiectomies
slicing away their bits
for anonymity, uniformity

Your beautiful bottoms
cast in white pure porcelain
aesthetically profound
framed in a square, lined along a wall
carry no hint
of the angst they cause

The folds and flaps, the twisting hairs
on mounds of venus
I asked him, my new man
'Anyone you know?'
Wondering if a man would recognise
those other lips of his woman.

Valeria Ramirez

Who?

Once you hitchhiked all the way to the border,
sometimes on the shoulders of your papa
sometimes in the arms of mama.
Hungry, tired, crabby
but holding hands of those you loved.
Times of walking, walking, walking
from all you knew in El Salvador
towards an el dorado.

You crossed the river
the massive Rio Grande.
Riding proud above the fear
of unnameable river monsters,
of the surging power of water
steadfast in the strength of your father's shoulders.

You stood there, wet, alone, on the bank
while he turned back for your mother.
Wailing, alone for the first time in weeks
needing the power of love
you leapt into the river to return to him.

Sure of his arms.

Still in the pouch he made of his T-shirt
to keep you safe and on his back
while he fought the current…
there you lie, silent
face down in the river
moving only with muddy eddies.

And now you hitchhike
on our conscience
riding the guilt we fear to feel
in case we acknowledge our cruelty.

Your photo on every TV
and every newspaper

lying there, in the river.
Unknown, uncounted
and unnamed to us
until you were dead.

Small-town Girl

She was shunned by most of us
and the story as we thought we knew it
passed on indiscreetly
with scarcely contained glee in the relief
that it was her, not us.

She was burnt you know.
She was only five, and her parents left her burning in the house
after they escaped.

Her folks never called out, never told them
but the firemen found her curled up near the door.

A little kid, she'd fallen asleep in front of the fire
until she was   fire.

And now she wears that melted face
with one eye glaring at the world
her single knuckled stumps grasp tightly to what she wants.

She's refused surgery you know
she wants us all to see she was left to burn.

And you know those kids she's got?
Well the boys get her pissed up the top pub, and have a bet
to see if they can get her to put a bag on her head
before they'll fuck her.

She's got three kids that way.
No fella.
She wouldn't even know who it was.

Wouldn't you think she'd do something about it?
Looking like that?

She must still
feel the screaming.
Her hands reaching   for someone   anyone
until her fingers burnt away.

Change of Heart

Those bloody starlings
Each year, same place, same time
the starlings invade roof space.
Sneaking under eaves, poking into corners
pulling at loose boards on old farmhouses
and crapping on the clean windows
of suburban triple-fronteds
manicured lawn and all.

A beautiful bird, a spangled, sparkly,
sequined dinner dressed bird
defies all logic,
dragging long strands of hay and twine,
spiderweb and grass
till the stolen space is full of jumbled nest.

Those bloody starlings
each year, same place, same time
the old farmer climbs the ladder
to foil the birds.
Drags nests and eggs asunder
drops them in the rubbish
and stops the hole again,
again with wire mesh

The bloody starlings
he mutters under breath
started early this year, the buggers.
Reaching from his ladder
he drags a handful of hay
and in his hand lies
a scrap of bulging belly
stretched wide mouth
And pulsing heart
Beat Beat Beating.

And for his own heartbeat
Beat Beat
he pauses,
then throws it in the rubbish
with the straw, the hay, the care

And climbs down the ladder.

But for weeks after
sometimes he can feel
that beating heart in his hand.

Claire Anne Taylor

As striking as a Viking
she strides along the stage
strong jaw framed with autumn hair
artist's hands hold a guitar
which fits her body like a soul mate.
Long long legs coloured by black tights
stretch into well worn cowboy boots.

And then   she starts to sing
and an ancestry of smoky whisky
all the potato famine victims
all the troubles and conquered souls of Erin
whose blood flows through her veins
wailing their loss through the years
permeates the air.

And yet she sings of here
of her homeland, not her bloodland.
She sings of her brothers
and the fireplace her father built.
She sings of her mother's strength
and the bush that nurtured her
in her ageless, otherworldly voice.

And the hairs on my neck rise
with the presence
of the years and lives past
that are also
standing here
listening to her song

Home

A huge desert sky, our
campfire bloods the darkness.

I turn away, and seek, as always
the southern cross,
high overhead
pointing the way home

About the Author

Rees Campbell is a proud and passionate Tasmanian woman who is inspired by the island she was lucky enough to be born on, and writes about the extraordinary people, places, creatures and plants she shares it with. Love in all its seasons and place in all its intricacies are the arteries that drive Rees's poems.

Rees lives in Wynyard at Murnong Wild Food Garden with her husband, Col, and poodle Darci, where she grows, prepares and promotes Tasmania's edible native plants…and they also spend time enjoying their mountain conservation property.

Rees has four previous books: *A Thousand Pleasures, A Million Treasures*, a beachcomber's guide to the Tasmanian coast; *The Legacy*, a fictionalised autobiography; *Brazenly Pure*, a genre-bending mix of poetry, essays, photography and children's art; and *Eat Wild Tasmanian*, the first book on the edible native plants of Tasmania. Her poetry and short stories have appeared in a number of anthologies.

A Thousand Pleasures, A Million Treasures: 'What a find to discover a book that is so approachable and yet so informative. I take it with me every beach walk.' ST

The Legacy: 'You write with great clarity and confidence. I am hungry to read more so look forward to your next book, I love your writing style and *The Legacy* is by far the best read I have had in years.' JM

Brazenly Pure: 'The book is fabulous. I don't believe I have ever seen such a fantastic collection of nature poems.' RS

Eat Wild Tasmanian: '*Eat Wild Tasmanian* is an absolutely fantastic book. Cannot put it down. Life-changing.' KL

www.ingramcontent.com/pod-product-compliance
Lightning Source LLC
Chambersburg PA
CBHW062154100526
44589CB00014B/1837